INDIA
the people

Bobbie Kalman

The Lands, Peoples, and Cultures Series

Crabtree Publishing Company

The Lands, Peoples, and Cultures Series
Created by Bobbie Kalman

Written by
Bobbie Kalman
Margaret Hoogeveen
Christine Arthurs

Editor-in-Chief
Bobbie Kalman

Editors
Margaret Hoogeveen
Christine Arthurs

Design
Heather Delfino

Pasteup
Adriana Longo

Printer
Worzalla Publishing Company
Stevens Point, Wisconsin

Illustrations
Halina Below-Spada: Back cover
Renée Mansfield: p. 8-9

Photography acknowledgments
Cover: Jeremy Ferguson/First Light
Tony Stone Worldwide/Masterfile: p.7; Chris Beeman: p.17(bottom, right);
Mary Bredin: p.21(right); Ian Clifford/E-Side Studios: p.16, 27; Bev Dywan: p.11(top), 24;
Ken Faris: Title page, p.5, 25, 31(top); Catriona Gordon: p.12(top and bottom), 19, 21(left), 30;
Ron Hayes: p.29; Susan Hughes: p.15(top and bottom), 23;
Sudha & Abdullah Khandwani: p.4, 11(bottom, left); Eric Melis: p.31(bottom);
Larry Rossignol: p.11(bottom, right), 20, 22; Pamela Sayne: p.28;
Mike Silver: p.17(top and bottom left), 18; Shiv Sud: p.14.

For Christine and Marni

The Indian man on the cover is wearing a colorful turban, as do many men in India. The motif that appears in the heading of every section represents the wheel of Ashoka, part of the Indian flag. The stylized peacock on the back cover shows the magnificence of India's national bird.

Cataloguing in Publication Data

Kalman, Bobbie, 1947-
    India, the people

(Lands, peoples, and cultures series)
Includes index.

ISBN 0-86505-211-5 (bound) ISBN 0-86505-291-3 (pbk.)
1. India - social conditions - 1947-   -
Juvenile literature. I. Title. II. Series.

HN683.5.K35 1990   j954   LC93-30923

Published by
Crabtree Publishing Company

350 Fifth Avenue	360 York Road, RR 4,	73 Lime Walk
Suite 3308	Niagara-on-the-Lake,	Headington,
New York	Ontario, Canada	Oxford OX3 7AD
N.Y. 10118	L0S 1J0	United Kingdom

Contents

5   Living in harmony

6   India's ancient history

8   Building a new nation

10   The many faces of India

14   Family life

16   Homes

18   Village life

20   Living in the city

22   Languages and education

24   Occupations

26   Social problems

28   The cycle of poverty

30   Indian ways

32   Glossary & Index

Living in harmony

India is a large Asian country with the second-highest population in the world. Over eight hundred million citizens share a common history that dates back 4500 years. Some of these people are Hindu, others Muslim; some farm, others study; some speak Gujarat, others Tamil. Despite the great variety of lifestyles and customs, Indians try to accept the differences among their various groups in order to live together peacefully. Indian people are tolerant of one another because their bonds are stronger than their differences.

Although the people of India are part of an ancient culture, the independent country of India is young. Its government is working hard to build a nation that will provide all its citizens with food, shelter, education, and employment. For any country, these needs are difficult to meet. For India, a less-developed nation, it is even more difficult. India is burdened with a tremendous population and many serious problems. The people of India's strong sense of national pride, however, will help them realize their goals.

(opposite) The people of India have much to smile about.

(below) India must work hard to protect both young and old from poverty. This grandfather and grandaughter share a quiet moment together.

Indian civilization began about 2500 B.C. in a valley along the Indus River, from which India gets its name. The people who lived there were called the Dravidians. Around a thousand years later the Aryans, a nomadic people from the northwest, invaded the Indus Valley and forced the Dravidians to move farther south. The Aryans settled in the valley and eventually all over the country. Over the years their ways and customs were blended together with those of the Dravidians to form the unique culture of India. One outcome of the combination of these two peoples was the flourishing of the Hindu religion. Their common faith firmly united the two peoples.

Spokes of peace

Over its long history India was invaded by many foreigners and ruled by emperors, *rajas*, *shahs*, and *sultans*. The nation was first united for a time in the fourth century B.C. during the Mauryan Empire. At that time Emperor Ashoka converted to Buddhism, a religion opposed to killing. He became a kind-hearted leader who encouraged people of different faiths to live together peacefully. Today the many-spoked wheel of Ashoka is the symbol that appears on India's national flag. Just as the numerous spokes join together in the center to make a wheel, the different groups of people come together to form the country and culture of India.

Princely states

Throughout most of its early history India consisted of several states, each one ruled by a *raja*, or prince. *Rajas* were rich men who were the heads of powerful families. When one family ruled a large area and became very powerful, it was called a dynasty. The golden age of Indian art and science occurred in the fourth and fifth centuries during the Gupta dynasty.

(opposite) The beauty of the jewel-encrusted walls of Jaipur Palace gives us a glimpse of a time when powerful Indian princes ruled this magnificent land.

The Muslim empires

In 712 A.D. Muslim warriors invaded India's western borders. They wanted to spread the Islamic faith, a new religion that originated in the Arab countries. As a result, many Indians converted to Islam. In 1206 a Muslim army on agile horses finally conquered the Indian forces, which rode into battle on slow-moving elephants. A number of Muslim dynasties called the Delhi Sultanate then ruled India. The Sultan of Delhi was defeated in 1526 by Turkish Muslims. These conquerors formed the Mogul Empire, which ruled India for about two hundred years. Its leaders were called *shahs*.

European traders

In 1498 Vasco da Gama of Portugal was the first European to reach India by sailing around the southern tip of Africa. After the Portuguese, the Dutch, French, and British also came to trade with India. All these countries craved India's textiles, spices, and other luxury items. For many years they fought India and one another for trading privileges. A British company, called the East India Company, became the most successful trader and controlled most of India for many years.

The British Raj

Eventually India was made a colony of the British Empire in 1858. Under British rule India became a unified country. Railways and roads were built; postal and telegraph services were set up. The British Raj (*raj* means "rule") governed India without the consent of the Indian people. Being governed by foreigners made the Indians unhappy. They did not have the same rights or privileges as the British, nor were they allowed a say in how their country was run. Britain used India's raw materials, such as cotton, to make manufactured goods in its own factories. These goods were then sold back to the Indians. Producing goods in Britain increased Britain's wealth and prevented the growth of industry in India.

Building a new nation

For many centuries India was ruled by foreign powers. At the beginning of the twentieth century the people of India acquired a renewed pride in their heritage and a desire to be independent from Britain. Mohandas Karamachand Gandhi, a great leader, helped make this dream a reality. Gandhi believed that Britain had no right to rule India. He felt that Indians should govern their own country. The Indian people respected Gandhi's wise words and honored him with the title Mahatma, meaning "Great Soul."

Gandhi's peaceful struggle

Mahatma Gandhi taught that it is right to hate what is unjust but wrong to hate people. In the struggle for independence he did not want anyone to be killed, whether British or Indian. He believed in using non-violent ways to achieve India's goals. He encouraged Indians to refuse to buy British goods, quit British jobs, and start their own businesses. He also organized peaceful protests. Even when Gandhi was jailed for opposing Britain, he remained patiently dedicated to the struggle for independence. Gandhi's steadfast dedication inspired the Indian people to build a new nation.

The salt march

Gandhi's most successful protest was the salt march. For centuries Indians had collected their salt supplies directly from the sea. When the British Raj took over, the Indians were charged an unfair tax on salt that was produced in their own country. Gandhi decided to protest by collecting his own salt. The whole world watched as the old man and thousands of his followers walked twenty-six days to get to the ocean. At the seashore each person collected a handful of salt. This gesture of defiance demonstrated every Indian's desire for freedom.

Independence at last

Gandhi's efforts to bring self-rule to the country he loved were very effective. Britain was forced to grant India independence in 1947. Yet not all Indians were happy with the outcome. The Muslim minority was worried about being overpowered by the Hindu majority. This religious group wanted to form its own country. Gandhi and many others were against breaking up India. After much bloodshed it was decided that India would have to be divided. Two portions, one in the west and one in the east, were separated from India. Today they are known as Pakistan and Bangladesh.

The prime ministers

Jawaharlal Nehru became India's first prime minister. For many years he had worked closely with Mahatma Gandhi to gain India's independence from Britain. Nehru had a modern outlook and improved India's economy by promoting industrialization. Nehru's daughter, Indira Gandhi, was elected prime minister some time after her father's death. She became known as "Mother India" because she was such a powerful and popular leader. After Indira Gandhi was killed in 1984, her son, Rajiv Gandhi, became prime minister. He was succeeded, in turn, by V.P. Singh in 1989.

The government of India

The government of India is a democracy. In this type of system people elect representatives from political parties. In India these elected representatives become members of parliament. Parliament is the governing body that makes the laws. The head of parliament is the prime minister, who is the leader of the political party with the most elected members. He or she chooses officials to help run the government and has the responsibility of carrying out the laws of the land. India also has a president, who is appointed rather than elected.

Even though the majority of Indians have descended from the Dravidians and Aryans, the Indian population is made up of a whole variety of communities. The people of India may be grouped in many ways: by race, religion, language, region, and social position.

India's tribes

The original inhabitants of India, known as Adivasis, are not descendants of the Aryans and Dravidians. The Adivasis are a number of racial groups that lived in India before the Dravidians and Aryans settled there.

The Adivasis tribes once lived in the tropical jungles. When the forests were cleared for farmland, these people were forced to make their homes in the most remote areas of India. Today around fifty million Adivasis are scattered throughout the country. Some live in small, self-contained communities. They hunt and gather food and worship the forces of nature just as their ancestors did. They speak their own languages and remain apart from other Indians. Other Adivasis have joined Indian society. Members of the Koruba tribe, for example, have become *mahouts. Mahouts* are specialists that train and care for the elephants that are used in the lumbering industry.

Religious groups

People are sometimes grouped according to their religions. The majority of Indians are Hindu. Although Hindus live all over India, speak different languages, and belong to many racial groups, they all believe in a universal spirit called Brahman and follow similar traditions. About ten percent of India's population is Muslim. Muslims follow a religion called Islam. Sikhs, Parsis, Buddhists, Jews, Christians, and Jains make up the remaining portion of the population.

(opposite, top) Members of a Sikh community travel in the back of a truck on their way to a parade.

The Sikhs

The thirteen million Sikhs who live in India form a group that is bound together by their strong religious faith. The majority live in the state of Punjab in northern India. Sikhs believe in only one God and feel that people of every social class should be treated with equality.

The Sikhs have earned a reputation for being successful in business. Many hold positions as businessmen, doctors, engineers, pilots, and taxi drivers. Because their homeland in the Punjab is a flat and fertile plain, the Sikhs excel in agriculture. Using up-to-date farming technology, many Sikhs have become prosperous farmers.

Many different languages

Language is another way of grouping people. Over thousands of years many languages and dialects developed in India. Before modern means of transportation existed, few villagers traveled more than several kilometers from the place where they were born. As a result, each isolated area developed its own language and customs. Today there are fifteen officially recognized languages and over eight hundred dialects used in India.

The Tamils

The Tamils, who live in the southernmost state of India, share a strong sense of community because of their common language. In the state of Tamil Nadu, which means "the land of the Tamil," a vast majority of the people speak an ancient language similar to the language once spoken by the Dravidians.

The Tamils live in southern India, unaffected by Aryan and Muslim influences in the north. They have therefore been able to hold onto their cultural traditions. Most Tamils are Hindu. They have built many magnificent temples, which are fine examples of ancient Hindu art.

(above) This young Tamil is a descendant of the Dravidians.

(left) This girl is a member of one of the Adivasis tribes, the original inhabitants of India.

Regional differences

Some regions in India are inhabited by distinct groups. Sometimes a whole group of people with already-established customs moved to India and settled in one particular area. For instance, the Parsis fled Persia to live in India. Today most Parsis reside in and around the city of Bombay.

Sometimes different peoples settled in one area. Over time their customs blended, and new ways emerged. Today these communities have their own distinctive cultures. The Kashmiris all live in one region and have established a unique community. Most Kashmiris are Muslim, but no Muslim community is quite like the Kashmiri community.

(left) The people who live in the mountainous region of Ladakh have a culture unique in India.

(below) This young Kashmiri girl drapes the end of her sari over her head, as is the custom of Muslim women.

The Kashmiris

The Kashmiris live in picturesque valleys in northernmost India. Unlike the rest of the country, this area receives snow in winter. Many people in Kashmir live on houseboats on the Jhelum River, which flows through the region. The first houseboats were built because a local law stated that only Kashmiris could own land. Europeans and other Indians who wanted to settle there found a spot on the river and used their boats as homes. Soon this became common among Kashmiris, too.

Many Kashmiris are fruit growers. In winter months they produce beautiful handicrafts. Using willow wood, they weave baskets, lampshades, chairs, and tables. They make carpets from brightly colored threads of wool and cotton. Kashmiris are also well known for their embroidery, jewelry, wood carving, pâpier-maché, and shawls.

The Ladakhi people

Located in the foothills of the Himalayas, Ladakh is one of the highest inhabited places in the world. The people of Ladakh are strong and hardy because they have to survive a cold climate and rugged landscape. The main crop grown by Ladakhi farmers is barley. Shepherds called *changpas* follow their flocks from pasture to pasture. The big, shaggy yak is important to the ancient Ladakhi way of life. Yaks are able to carry heavy loads over the rough mountain terrain. Their long hair is woven into mats and used to make tents called *ribos*. Yaks also provide milk, butter, and meat.

Division by caste

Most societies divide people into social classes in some way or another. For instance, in feudal societies there were kings and queens, lords and ladies, knights, and commoners. The Aryan people, who settled in India around 1500 B.C., separated people into four main groups called castes. The Brahmin were priests and scholars, the Kshatriya administrators and soldiers, the Vaishya artisans and merchants, and the Sudra farmers. People were also divided into thousands of subcastes according to their jobs or positions in life. Over the years the caste system became so rigid that people born into a certain caste remained there all their lives. They socialized and married only within their castes. Those who married outside their castes risked losing family and friends.

People followed the caste system because their religion, Hinduism, encouraged them to accept their stations in life. According to Hinduism each person has a *karma* that determines his or her position in society. *Karma* can be defined as fate or destiny. For instance, if you are born a grocer, it is your destiny to remain a grocer as long as you live. *Karma* makes it difficult for you to improve your life by making you feel you should not change it.

The "children of god"

People outside the caste system were once called "untouchables." These unfortunate people occupied such a low position in society that other Hindus did not want to come anywhere near them. The "untouchables" were the poorest members of Indian society and were required to perform the worst jobs.

Mahatma Gandhi campaigned to improve the lives of the untouchables. He gave them the new name Harijan, which means the "children of God." To demonstrate his sincere belief that all people are equal, he took up a broom and began sweeping the streets. No one but the Harijan were ever supposed to do this job. People gathered around him, shocked by his action. No public figure had ever challenged the caste system in this way. Gandhi asked, "How can India be free if all Indians are not free?"

Traditions are hard to break

The Indian government has outlawed the caste system because it was so unfair. It is trying to make up for the problems caused by the old system. For example, a university education is now possible for many Harijans. Tradition is often hard to break, however, and many people still follow the rules of the caste system.

 # Family life

The joint family

The traditional Indian family is called a joint family. A joint family includes parents, children, aunts, uncles, and grandparents. When a man marries, he and his wife remain in the home of his parents. When a woman gets married, she must leave home to join her husband and his parents. In India it is not unusual to find four generations of a joint family living under one roof. In villages it is still common for twelve or more family members to share accommodation.

The all-important marriage

A wedding is a very important event in the Indian family because marriage is considered to be the union of two families. Traditionally, parents search for suitable marriage partners for their children from members of their own caste. Partners in arranged marriages often come together as strangers and later grow to love each other. Although most Indian marriages are still arranged, there are also some "love marriages." A love marriage occurs when two people fall in love and then marry each other.

(above) A traditional wedding is a family celebration.

The men of the house

In the Indian household the men are in charge of the family. They make most of the major decisions and enjoy positions of privilege and respect. The oldest male, usually the grandfather, holds the highest position. All men must earn a living to support their sometimes huge families. Sons inherit the family land or business from their father and all the duties that go along with it. The greatest duty of sons is to provide for their parents in their old age.

Women's responsibilities

Women are responsible for the household. In the villages they wake up very early to get started on the long day's work. Most have few modern conveniences, so taking care of the home is a full-time job. At dawn women often begin their day by pounding wheat into flour. Clothes must be washed by hand, food cooked over an open fire, and water carried from community wells. All these chores make the working day very long. Besides caring for husband, children, and parents-in-law, many women also toil hard in the fields.

In recent years many women have become professionals who hold jobs outside the home. Women are now being trained as scientists, doctors, and teachers. Only women from well-to-do families, however, have the chance to pursue such careers.

Hope for the children

Children are the center of the Indian household and receive much attention from their loving families. Couples are especially happy when a boy is born. A son, along with his wife, will care for his parents when they become old. Parents try to educate their children and hope that they will live healthy, happy, and prosperous lives. Many children are now better educated than their parents. If a family is poor, however, children often go to work at a young age to help support the family. India hopes that in the future all children will go to school.

Bilal's family

Bilal, a ten-year-old Kashmiri boy, lives on a houseboat with his family. Their boat is on Lake Nagan in the state of Jammu and Kashmir. The family stays on the boat all year long—even in winter when it snows! Along with his parents and grandparents Bilal lives with his sisters Muna and Shadys and his baby brother Julany.

Only Bilal goes to school. Every morning, after he gets dressed in his uniform, his grandmother takes him across the lake. After school, Bilal has many chores to do. Sometimes he takes his family shopping in a small boat called a *shikara*. He also pumps up water from the lake for his mother. In winter he shovels the snow that has collected on the roof of the houseboat. When the chores are done, Bilal likes to fish off the end of the boat or go swimming with his friends. In the evening the family gathers to listen to the radio. When it gets dark, they roll out a big mattress and everyone falls asleep to the sound of water lapping gently against the side of the boat.

(top) Bilal and a friend go fishing with Bilal's father. They do not travel far from their houseboat homes.

(right) Later Bilal's mother prepares a tasty fish supper with the day's catch.

Although sometimes made of bricks or pink sandstone, most village houses are constructed from a mixture of clay, straw, and cow dung. After this mixture has dried, it is very hard. Thick walls help keep out the summer heat. Some families whitewash the walls to reflect the sun's hot rays. Even so, homes are often so stuffy inside that people prefer to sleep under the stars in the cool night breeze. In some regions homes are built with flat roofs, so family members can sleep on top of their houses. Most homes have only two rooms and perhaps an enclosed courtyard where the animals are kept.

Furniture

The average Indian home has few pieces of furniture. Some shelves or storage bins may line a wall, and floor mats made of jute provide places for people to sit. The most important piece of furniture in the Indian home is a bed called a *charpoy*. A *charpoy* is a frame with a mat across the top woven out of rope. During the day people sit on it or else lean it against a wall. On warm evenings it is taken outside.

The kitchen

The corner of one room serves as a kitchen area. Food is cooked on a sunken stove or a portable clay stove. Wood or dried cow dung is used as fuel. There are only a few supplies: some pots and pans, utensils, and a flat pan for cooking *chapatis*. Foodstuffs are stored in baskets or brass pots. Often the legs of large bins are set into little bowls of water so that insects cannot climb up the legs and get into the food supply.

The floor is kept very clean because cooks traditionally prepare meals while crouching or sitting on the floor. Instead of a knife, a woman uses a *bonthi*, which is a sharp blade mounted on the floor. She pares and slices vegetables and carves meat on it if her family is not vegetarian. The floor is washed thoroughly every night. The water runs down a drain in the middle of the room. A traditional Indian family eats seated on the floor in a big circle. It is considered a courtesy to allow the men to eat first.

A woman and her mother-in-law prepare the evening meal. Here they make some Indian-style bread.

The family shrine

Essential to the traditional Hindu home is a small space or alcove for a shrine. Here the family keeps a picture or statue of the family's favorite deity. The image is frequently washed and decorated with garlands of flowers and incense. Before meals the family makes symbolic offerings of food to the statue. These rituals of worship are called *puja*. Family members pray that their deity will bring them health and good fortune.

(above) Homes vary from region to region. These desert homes are built with bricks made from local materials.

(below, left) Only the wealthy can afford to live in modern suburban neighborhoods such as this.

(below) The all-purpose **charpoy** *is the most essential piece of furniture in the average Indian home.*

Over three quarters of India's population live in villages scattered across the country. Many of these communities consist of small clusters of houses nestled together, whereas some large villages have thousands of inhabitants. Generally, families live close to one another and share a strong sense of community with their neighbors. The houses in most villages are built around a square where everyone gathers in the evening. An elected group of elders, called the *panchayat*, meets here from time to time to make decisions concerning village matters. Beyond the village lies the farmers' fields.

Few modern conveniences

The average village home has few modern conveniences. Running water, indoor toilets, washing machines, refrigerators, hair dryers, and air-conditioners are all items that the average Indian family does without. Many families do have portable radios, however, and most have access to television at the local community center. In recent times more and more villages are being supplied with electricity.

At the edge of the village square, men of the community meet to exchange stories and pass the time.

These women get water by lowering jugs deep into the village well. The well is a hub of activity.

The center of village life

The well is the center of daily life in an Indian village. It provides everyone with water for drinking, cooking, bathing, and cleaning. Well water is also used to water the fields. Water buffalo or oxen are often used to haul the water up from the well. In the past most wells in India were open. In order to fill their jugs, people walked down a few steps right into the water. This made the water dirty and caused sickness to be easily spread. Disease-carrying insects also thrived in open wells. Now most villages have covered wells, which have greatly reduced the spread of disease. Many modern wells also have electric pumps.

Besides being a source of water, the local well is a center of social activity. When villagers go to the well to fetch water or do the laundry, they take the opportunity to visit with neighbors. Friends exchange the latest news and talk about all the things that make life interesting.

19

 # Living in the city

In India, as in other countries, city streets are busy and noisy places. Not only are they crowded with people and cars, they also teem with rickshaws and cows, street vendors and performers. People rush to get to work. Others beg passersby for a little change. Some do a little shopping. Instead of big department stores, there are small shops, outdoor booths, and merchandise spread out for sale on carpets on the ground. Books, kitchen utensils, medicine, spices, sweets, and a countless number of other items are available in the city streets.

The city also provides many types of entertainment. People often go to the movies or take part in outdoor games and sports. Middle-class families belong to clubs and dine at restaurants. Cities are the cultural centers of India, offering their residents museums, art galleries, historic sights, and theaters.

City slums
Because cities are growing at such a fast rate, there is a drastic housing shortage in India. One third of the city dwellers cannot find or afford accommodation, so they must live in tents or shacks crowded together in slums. Many others sleep on the street. Street people can be seen curled up at the sides of buildings and in alleyways on make-shift beds. The people in slums or on the streets do not have toilets or clean water. A large number of the poorest city dwellers originally came from small villages to find employment. Because they can only find low-paying jobs or no jobs at all, they cannot afford to rent apartments or rooms.

(above) The streets of India's cities are always filled with people going about their daily business.

Many Indians live in crowded apartment buildings.

City apartments

Those fortunate enough to have somewhere to call home usually live in small apartments with several relatives. A common type of apartment building is called a *chawl*. A *chawl* has three to six stories, with twenty or more one-room apartments on each floor. There are no separate kitchens or living rooms in these apartments. The tenants on each floor share a bathroom at the end of the hall. Sometimes there is not enough room for the whole family, so some family members sleep on the street. They come home to eat and have their laundry done.

A fortunate middle class

Although many city dwellers are poor, the city is also the home of a growing middle class. Many people who live in cities have good jobs and make a good living. Some families have spent generations in the city, often renting or owning the same home for decades. These families live comfortably with adequate space and facilities. They pay to send their children to private schools and hire servants to help with household chores or to drive the family car. A washerman calls every day to pick up the family's dirty laundry. Vendors come right to the door to sell vegetables, spices, or textiles. Although many men work away from home, they still prefer their wives' cooking. A special service transports a home-cooked meal to a hungry husband just in time for lunch.

This man cannot find a place to live so he sleeps on the street with his pet monkey. The growing number of homeless people is a major problem in Indian cities.

City problems

Although only twenty percent of India's population lives in the cities, urban centers are extremely overcrowded. Only the wealthy and upper-middle classes enjoy good living conditions. Each year millions of people flock to the cities to find work, but there are not nearly enough jobs for everyone. As a result, crime is on the increase.

Solving city problems is an enormous task. The Indian government has trouble meeting the basic needs of its population and does not have the money or equipment to handle other problems. A few projects, however, are under way. For instance, some cities have started to clean up the slum areas and supply them with clean water and public toilets.

Languages and education

Sometimes Indians have a hard time understanding one another. From region to region, and sometimes from village to village, people speak different languages or dialects. Areas developed their own languages because villages and towns used to be isolated from one another. Without planes, trains, or cars most people passed their whole lives without ever meeting a person from outside the area around their village.

Fifteen distinct languages and over eight hundred dialects are used in India. Languages in the north developed from Sanskrit, the ancient language of the Aryans. Languages in the south developed from the original language of the Dravidians. Some languages use entirely different alphabet systems. This makes it difficult for people to learn one another's languages.

A common language

To help solve communication problems, the government made Hindi the official language of the country. Although Hindi is the mother tongue of less than half the population, it is now being taught in every school. Knowledge of the English language also helps bridge the communication gap. English is used in universities, government, science, and business.

Reading and writing skills

In India the rate of illiteracy—sixty-four percent—is one of the highest in the world. Special allowances are made for those who cannot read or write. Many signs use pictures instead of words. Voting cards, for example, use the symbols of the political parties so that people who cannot read are still able to vote.

People who are illiterate have a difficult time getting by. It is nearly impossible for them to get jobs other than manual labor. Even finding their way to an unfamiliar place is a challenge for those who cannot read. India is trying to provide everyone with reading and writing skills.

Public education

The government is attempting to make basic education available to everyone by providing free education. To help provide the materials needed for schooling, the government has launched "Operation Blackboard." This program has helped supply villages with school buildings and teachers. A slate and chalk are often used as learning tools. Unlike paper, a slate can be used again and again. Books are often in short supply.

Some parents send their children to private schools, which are modeled on British schools. Only parents who can afford to pay the yearly fees can send their children to these schools. Some private schools are run by religious institutions such as Christian missions.

Work or school?

In rural areas it is difficult to keep children at school when they are needed to work on the farm. In cities many children help their parents earn a living instead of going to school. Sometimes girls stay at home to do housework or look after younger brothers and sisters. If only one child can be spared to go to school, a son is given the first chance. With so many responsibilities, many children cannot finish their schooling even when it is available.

Going to school

Indian children start school at the age of six. In villages they get up early in the morning to walk to school. If the weather is good, lessons are held in the shade of a tree rather than in the stuffy classroom. Everyone sits cross-legged on the ground in neat rows, the boys on one side, girls on the other.

(opposite) Village schools have few supplies and poor facilities, but students are eager to learn.

When it gets too hot and stuffy in the classroom, students learn their lessons in the shady schoolyard.

Some classrooms have desks, especially in the city schools. The teacher instructs students to read and write in their native language, as well as in Hindi. Students also learn mathematics, Indian history, and geography. They often chant their lessons out loud. Everyone enjoys a two-month summer vacation.

Children are supposed to stay in school until they are fourteen years of age. They attend primary and middle school and some go on to high school. They have final exams at the end of the tenth grade and another set in the twelfth grade to prepare for college or university. To gain entry into university, students must speak, read, and write in English. Many universities and hundreds of technical colleges are now open. As a result, more and more students can acquire professions or learn skills and trades. The most popular professions are in medicine, engineering, and agriculture.

About three quarters of India's people make their living from the land, but there are many other types of jobs in India. Industries and factories employ thousands of people. Some work for the government; others run small businesses of their own. Until recently Indians did not have much choice regarding how they could earn a living. Most people worked at the same jobs as those of their fathers. Today, because of higher education and new technology, a larger variety of job opportunities is available.

The family business

Most boys are trained by their fathers to carry on the family trade. A farmer's son learns all about the land. A goldsmith's son learns the skill of crafting delicate gold jewelry. A boy usually helps his father in the family business until his father is ready to retire. Then he takes on the business himself and supports his aging parents. Later on he teaches his own son the family trade.

India's cottage industry

Indians have always owned and run cottage industries. Cottage industries are small businesses conducted in people's homes. In large villages artisans and workers provided goods and services such as jewelry, batik, leather work, blacksmithing, and weaving to the rest of the community.

When India began to industrialize, many cottage-industry owners suffered. People started to buy factory-made goods instead of items made within the community. To counter this trend, Mahatma Gandhi encouraged Indians to start more cottage industries. He hoped that these small businesses would enable people to stay in their villages and create self-sufficient communities. Today centers called *ashrams* teach valuable skills to local people so they can set up their own small businesses. Cottage industries now flourish throughout India.

Outdoor stalls offer a wide range of services for both village and city dweller. Attracted by a huge model of the human jaw, many passersby stop to have their teeth checked and fixed.

The lure of the city

Many young people must leave their villages because there is not enough land for farming or there are too many people employed in the same trades. Some of these people look forward to new lives, whereas others do not want to leave their homes. Most of them go to the cities looking for work. They soon discover that millions of other people are hoping to find jobs in the city, too. Many of these unemployed people never find jobs. Others end up in low-paying jobs working as rickshaw drivers, household servants, and construction workers.

The bonding bind

Some people end up as bonded laborers. A bonded laborer is someone who works for a money lender in order to pay back a debt. Money lenders pay very low wages and charge their workers large sums of money for the use of equipment and services, including transportation to and from the work site. The employee is forced to continue working because he or she can never save enough money to pay back the original debt.

Bonded labor has been outlawed by the government but continues because many people have never been informed of their rights. Some unscrupulous employers even tell their workers that their debts must be passed on to their children. Five million people are still trapped in this never-ending cycle of bonded labor and poverty.

A privileged few

University educations and well-paying professional jobs are available to only a small number of Indians. It costs a great deal of money to attend university. Professionals such as engineers, scientists, and lawyers often come from privileged backgrounds. Today the government has programs that give underprivileged people the chance to attend university and become professionals. As a result, more and more young people will be able to further their education, get better jobs, and improve their living conditions.

In India many men and women work at manual labor. The work day is long and exhausting, little attention is paid to safety, and employees have no job security.

Social problems

The Indian government has a great responsibility. It must guide the development of India's economy to ensure that all citizens are able to support themselves and their families. To achieve this worthy goal the government has encouraged industrial development. Unfortunately there are many other social problems that burden the people of India.

Overflowing with people

The population of India is growing at a high speed. Every year it increases by about two percent. At this rate, by the middle of the next century India will have more people than any other country in the world, including China. It is highly unlikely that India will be able to support this huge population. The country already has great difficulty providing food, housing, education, health care, and jobs for all its citizens. Overpopulation is probably the greatest problem facing India today.

The money gap

In India there has always been a huge gap between the very rich and the very poor. Indian princes, whose families once ruled India, possess huge family fortunes. A small number of merchant families have also become rich in the business world. These people live in luxury. A new middle class has recently emerged, however, due to increased industry. Middle-class families can afford to live fairly comfortable lives. Unfortunately, a much larger number of people have no money at all. With the population of India growing by leaps and bounds, many more people are born into a life of poverty every year. India must do something to close the gap between the rich and poor.

A lack of jobs

A large number of Indians have a difficult time making a living. Many people are unemployed because there are simply not enough jobs for everyone. Others can find work, but not doing what they have been trained to do. These people are underemployed. At one time they studied hard at college or university, with the hope of entering a career of their choice. They soon discover that the positions they want are already filled. In order to make a living, they accept low-paying jobs. An architect, for instance, might drive a taxi instead of designing buildings because he is desperate for work. These working conditions cause many highly trained people to leave India so they can follow their chosen careers.

The case against caste

For centuries Indian society was divided into castes. A caste determines a person's place in society. Although the caste system has been outlawed by the government, many people still follow its traditional rules. As a result, a person of low caste finds it extremely difficult to improve his or her situation in life. Imagine what it would be like if you belonged to a caste responsible for cleaning washrooms. Even if you were intelligent, hard-working, and of good character, you would still be expected to clean toilets for the rest of your life.

Women with little say

While their brothers go off to school, many girls look after their younger brothers and sisters or help their mothers with housework. These girls never learn to read or write. Without an education they never experience the joy of learning and have a hard time getting good jobs when they grow up. Most Indian women work from dawn to dusk trying to keep their households going. Some work outside the home as well. Although they often have to do the toughest jobs, such as carrying gravel at construction sites, they usually get paid the lowest wages. No matter how hard they work, women are always expected to eat only after everyone else has had their fill. Because of their low position in society, most Indian women lack power and freedom.

Unhealthy conditions

Poor sanitation is the cause of many health problems in India. Disease and infection spread quickly in unsanitary conditions. People get sick with dysentery because they must drink dirty water. Many regions are without public toilets, so human waste is left in the streets. This increases the spread of disease because germs get into the air, the water, and onto people. During the monsoon season the air is hot and extremely humid. Everything is covered with a thin film of water. Germs multiply and spread in these damp conditions. People get sick easily because they are constantly wet. Today Indians receive better health care than ever before. Far fewer people die from tuberculosis, leprosy, malaria, or dysentery, but these diseases are still a serious problem in India.

(above) Slums have become a part of the landscape in India's cities. People put together make-shift homes of cardboard, tar paper, plastic sheets, or corrugated metal. Daily life goes on as people cook, wash, work, and raise animals such as the two goats in this picture.

A suffering environment

Since independence, the Indian government has encouraged industrialization. Unfortunately, rapid industrialization has caused serious damage to the environment. The destruction of the environment affects every person's life. People get diseases from polluted water. They cannot avoid the smell of garbage and human waste because neither are disposed of properly. They can consume dangerous chemicals when pesticides or chemical fertilizers are used to raise crops. Air pollution causes breathing problems. To ensure a healthy future, the Indian government must create and enforce laws to protect the environment.

Getting things done

It is sometimes difficult to get things done in India because companies and government agencies are often poorly run. Information is not organized, so mounds of paper fill up office space. To accomplish anything, you probably need to fill out several forms and stand in two or three long lineups.

 # The cycle of poverty

Shanti smiled at her husband, Dipu, who waved to her from his bicycle rickshaw. It was getting late in the afternoon, and Shanti had not yet sold all her lemons. She sat cross-legged at the side of the road, a heap of lemons beside her. Knowing that her boss would be displeased if she did not sell them soon, Shanti called out to the people walking nearby, "Lemons for sale! Good, fresh lemons. Come and get your lemons."

Shanti's throat felt sore from calling out to customers all day long. Just before dawn she had been awakened by the cries of her daughter Devi. Devi needs Shanti's constant attention because she is sick with diarrhea. Shanti came out of the tent to make a little breakfast and tea for Dipu. As she used up the last of the flour to make *chapatis,* she wondered if she would earn enough money by the end of the day to buy food for the family and medicine for Devi.

Shanti got married at the age of sixteen. Before the wedding day, her parents had told her that her future husband would be able to buy her a new house. Her father and mother arranged her marriage to Dipu, a boy from another village. He was the son of a brick maker. Dipu's two older brothers had already entered their

father's business, so Dipu did not have a job. Soon after baby Devi was born, the young husband and wife set out for Bombay to find work and a new place to live.

When Shanti and Dipu reached Bombay, they marveled at the sights. Dipu noticed the double-decker buses, and Shanti was fascinated by the movie theaters. She imagined how wonderful it would be to work as a ticket seller, but she knew that she was not dressed well enough to apply for a position. The pair did not have enough money to see the movie, but Dipu promised Shanti that someday they would go to the movies together.

The couple had a hard time finding work. Dipu only knew the trade of brick making, and Shanti had only attended school for three years. Dipu finally found a job with a taxi company. While he rides customers around the city on a bicycle rickshaw, Shanti sells lemons on the street for a local farmer. Although they both work, their income is so small that they can barely afford to feed themselves. The young family lives in a tent in the slums of Bombay.

(above) Despite their poverty, Shanti, Dipu, and Devi enjoy the times they spend together.

An old story

The story of Shanti and Dipu is not a happy one. It is typical of millions of people in India who live without the basic necessities of life. Poor people must struggle to survive with inadequate food, shelter, education, and health care. Like millions of others, Shanti and Dipu are trapped in the cycle of poverty. They earn just enough to get by, but not enough to improve their situation. Higher wages would make it possible for them to save a little money, and low-rent apartments would provide them with a place to live. Public education would help Devi get a job when she grows up. These solutions are very difficult to attain.

A symposium on poverty

How is the plight of Shanti and Dipu similar to the plight of poor people all over the world? What are some of the causes of poverty? Why does poverty seem like a circle without an end? Think of at least ten hurdles homeless people must face when they try to better their situations. Why might it be more difficult to break the cycle of poverty in some countries than in others? How can governments help people better their positions in life?

Hold a symposium on poverty. Interview a welfare officer in your city or town or invite him or her to your school. Find out about the real problems poor families face and why it is so difficult for them to improve their situations.

Global feast and famine

Hold a global lunch in your classroom or cafeteria. Ask thirty people to take part, make sure twenty are hungry, but do not give them any details about the lunch. Serve thirteen people a cup of rice and a glass of water. Give four people a bowl of rice, a serving of vegetables, and a glass of water. Three people will receive appetizers, soup, meat, vegetables, bread, dessert, chocolates, and a large milkshake. There should also be an audience of at least ten people who have had lunch beforehand. Provide these spectators with paper and pencils and ask them to record any conversations.

Dipu must take his bath at a water pump in the street. Poor people do without the facilities that most of us take for granted.

Now proceed with the lunch. Do people argue about the food they are given? Does anyone complain? How many people share? What role do the spectators play? In the real world, who might the spectators be?

This type of lunch shows the gap between the rich and poor around the world. More than two thirds of the world's population receive only a tiny bit to eat each day. About one quarter is fed a little more. Ten percent, however, eat. much more than they need. These people also have a greater choice concerning what they eat. In which group do you belong? After explaining the facts above to the participants, ask the students what conclusions they have reached. Are there any ways that they, as individuals, can make a difference in the real world?

A happy ending?

Write an ending for Shanti and Dipu's story. Have your friends do the same. Do you think Shanti and Dipu would be happy with your endings? Discuss whether your solutions are practical. What do you think the future really holds for this couple and their children? Do you think Shanti and Dipu can be happy even when they are poor? What makes you happy?

Indian ways

The colors of India

An ever-present dazzling use of color reflects the artistic flair of India's people. Houses are often painted pastel pink, blue, or yellow. Multi-colored temples are decorated in great detail. Every market is a kaleidoscope of the luscious colors of fruits, flowers, and bright powdered dyes. Indian fabrics and clothes display every shade of the rainbow. Men wear colorful turbans on their heads. During the festival of *Holi*, everyone is covered in festive powders and dyes. Colors are not only attractive, they are also symbolic. Green stands for youth and life, red for happiness and joy, and blue for peace.

Fortune tellers

For thousands of years Indians have looked to the stars to guide their actions and predict the future. Astrology and fortune telling are both part of folk Hinduism. Astronomers are consulted before weddings are arranged and on other special occasions. Fortune tellers set up their wares in the bazaars. Some tell your fortune with the help of a bird!

Guess the Indian words

Many common words in the English language were originally Indian words. Here are ten: pajamas, bungalow, shampoo, cashmere, bazaar, thug, curry, tank, jodhpurs, mangos. Guess which words belong in each of the following sentences. Write the answers on a piece of paper—not in the book.

1. I like wearing my soft _ sweater.
2. A _ pushed the man down and took his money.
3. The mountie on the horse is wearing a hat, a red jacket, and a pair of _.
4. My grandmother lives in a _, so she does not have to climb up and down stairs.
5. In winter I wear cozy flannel _.
6. My friend Ritu bought a *sari* at a_.
7. The _ I use makes my hair squeaky clean.
8. _ are my favorite fruit.
9. Let's make a spicy _ for dinner!
10. Samantha does not like cleaning her fish _.

The Indian people love bright colors. During the **Holi** *festival they throw these powders at one another, creating an explosion of brilliant colors.*

Holy cow!

According to Hindu mythology, Brahma created Brahmins (priests) and cows at the same time. Cows are considered sacred, and dairy products such as milk and ghee (a type of butter) are used in religious ceremonies. It is forbidden by law to kill cows. Every year there is a festival called *Pongal* to honor these holy animals. During *Pongal*, people wash and decorate cows with colorful pastes and flower garlands.

Year-round yoga

Yoga is an example of a daily ritual that grew out of Hinduism. Yoga is used to help maintain a healthy body and mind. Yoga teachers, called yogis, practice yoga as a way of finding peace and spiritual fulfillment. Many people start each day with a series of yoga exercises called "A Salutation to the Sun." They say that doing this makes them feel great the whole day long. Go to your library and find a book on yoga. Try the sun salutation postures. They might make you feel excited about starting the day!

(above) The cow is special to Indian people. Cows are treated with great care and allowed to wander at will.

(below) A yogi greets another new day by saluting the sun at dawn.

Glossary

accommodation - A place to stay or sleep

artisan - A skilled craftsperson

astrology - The study of the positions of stars and planets and their influence on people's lives

Buddhism - A religion founded by Buddha, an ancient religious leader from India

caste system - An ancient Indian social system that classifies people according to birth

civilization - A society with a well-established culture that has existed for a long period of time

culture - The customs, beliefs, and arts of a distinct group of people

deity - A god or goddess

democracy - A form of government in which representatives are elected to make decisions for society

descendants - People who come from a particular family blood line

dialect - A way of speaking that differs from a standard language in some of its vocabulary, pronunciations, and sayings

dysentery - An infection of the intestine, which causes pain and severe diarrhea

economy - The way a country manages its money, goods, and services

generation - People born at about the same time. Grandparents, parents, and children make up three generations.

heritage - The customs, achievements, and history passed on from earlier generations; tradition

Hinduism - An ancient Indian religion based on the holy books called the *Vedas*

industrialization - The term used to describe a shift from an agricultural society to one that produces goods in factories

Islam - A religion founded by the prophet Muhammad. Its followers are called Muslims.

joint family - A family unit in which married sons remain in their parents' household

jute - The fiber from a jute plant used for making ropes and mats

leprosy - A disease that destroys the nerves, causing deformation and death

malaria - A disease that is spread by mosquitos, which breed in swamps and pools of water

modern conveniences - Up-to-date goods and services that make life easier, such as electricity and running water

monsoon - A rain-filled wind that blows inland from the ocean

parliament - A group of people that makes the laws for a country

pesticide - A chemical that is used to kill insects to prevent them from eating plants

pollution - Waste, such as chemicals and garbage, that harms the environment

race - A group of people who share similar physical characteristics that are passed along from generation to generation

raw material - A substance from the earth that is not yet processed or refined

sari - The traditional garment worn by many Indian women consisting of a long cloth wrapped around the waist and draped over the shoulder

symbol - Something that represents or stands for something else

symposium - A discussion of a certain topic

tolerance - A willingness to be patient towards people whose opinions and actions differ from one's own

tuberculosis - A deadly disease, caused by poor sanitation, that affects the lungs and bones

whitewash - To paint a thin white liquid on walls and other surfaces

Index

Adivasis 10, 11

artisans 13, 24

Aryans 6, 10, 13, 22

Bangladesh 8

British Empire 6, 8, 9

Buddhism 6, 10

caste system 13, 26

children 14, 15, 21, 23, 28, 29

cities **20-21**, 25, 28

cows 20, 31

Dravidians 6, 10, 11, 22

education 5, 15, 21, **22-23**, 24, 25, 26, 29

employment 5, 10, 13, 15, 20, 21, 23, **24-25**, 26, 28

families **14-15**, 16, 18, 20, 21, 24, 26, 28, 29

farming 10, 13, 18, 23, 25

food 5, 14, 16, 17, 21, 26, 28, 29

furniture 16, 17

Gandhi, Mahatma **8-9**, 13, 24

government 5, 9, 21, 25, 26, 27, 29

Harijan 13

health 19, 21, 26, 27, 28, 29

Hinduism 5, 6, 8, 10, 13, 17, 30, 31

history 5, **6-9**

homes 5, 13, 15, **16-17**, 18, 20, 21, 26, 27, 28, 29

industry 6, 9, 24, 26, 27

Islam 6, 10

Kashmiris 12, 13, 15

Ladakhis 12, 13

languages 5, 10, 22, 23, 30

marriage 14, 28

middle class 20, 21, 26

Muslims 5, 6, 8, 10, 12

Pakistan 8

Parsis 10, 12

people **10-13**

pollution 27

population 5, 10, 18, 21, 24, 26, 29

poverty 5, 21, 25, 26, **28-29**

prime ministers 9

problems 21, 25, **26-27**

religions 10, 12

salt march 8

Sikhs 10, 11

slums 20, 21, 27, 28

Tamils 5, 10, 11

villages **18-19**, 20, 22, 24, 28

water 14, 15, 18, 19, 20, 21, 27

weddings 14

wells 14, 19

3 4 5 6 7 8 9 WP Printed in U.S.A. 9 8 7 6 5